Arduino:

2020 Beginners Guide to Learn Arduino Programming . Amazing Projects included.

ARDUINO

Copyright © 2019

All rights reserved.

ISBN: 9781660614523

CONTENTS

Introduction..7

What is Arduino?..7

Why is the use of Arduino so popular?..10

Chapter 1: Advantages and disadvantages of Arduino....................14

Advantages:..14

Disadvantages:..16

Chapter 2: Types of Arduino Boards..20

1. Uno..24

2. Leonardo..27

3. ArdinoMega xxx...29

4. Arduino nano...31

5. Ardinomini..31

6. Compatible..34

7. What kind of Arduino is necessary to have at home?............39

Chapter 3: Arduino Mega Server..42

Arduino Serial Commander...43

APPLICATION AREA..44

1. Supported Web Technologies 47
2. Dynamic interface 48
3. Modern web technologies 48
4. Luxury conclusion 48
5. Change content on the fly 49
6. Adaptive design 49
7. Basic set 50
8. Fields of application 51

Chapter 4: Arduino IDE 55

What is Arduino IDE? 56

How to download and install Arduino IDE 58

Which version of the Arduino IDE to choose? 59

Download Arduino IDE from the official site 61

Arduino IDE Online 62

Chapter 5: Arduino projects that everyone must to try. 63

Arduino Microcontroller Process Automation Example 63

One of the projects to create a greenhouse using Arduino 65

Arduino microcontroller programming for process automation. Example 67

DIY thermal imager 69

RGB tape control from smartphone and Arduino 77

Arduino face recognition and tracking system 80

Dynamic (swivel) webcam on Arduino 86

Smart socket on the example of a teapot 92

Radio on Arduino 96

DIY crafts garland on address LEDs with your own hands 104

LED mood cube 110

Conclusion 118

ARDUINO

Thank you for purchasing this book!

We always try to give more value then you expect. That's why we've updated the content and you can get it for FREE. You can get the digital version for free because you bought the print version.

The book is under the match program from Amazon. You can find how to do this using next URL: https://www.amazon.com/gp/digital/ep-landing-page

I hope it will be useful for you.

Introduction

What is Arduino?

Arduino is a ready-made hardware and software platform, the main components of which are a small I / O controller board and a Processing / Wiring-based development environment.

The first prototype controller was released back in 2005 when Massimo Banzi developed it for students at the Institute for Interaction Design in Ivrea, Italy. The name of the device comes from the name of King Arduin, who ruled Italy for only two years at the beginning of the XI century, in whose honor the beer bar "di Re Arduino", owned by Massimo Banzi, was located and located on the same place where according to legend King Arduin was born.

Arduino's goal is to create an accessible environment for software developers that will allow them to enter the world of microcontroller programming. The programming of controllers of this company takes place in a simple and intuitive programming environment -

Arduino IDE. This environment is convenient for beginners as well as experienced users. The C ++ programming language is used, which is supplemented by many libraries, which simplifies the work with the device.

Arduino has revolutionized the world of electronic devices. Both schemes and source codes are available for free, which is why Arduino gained such wide popularity. The finished board can be purchased for just a few dollars, or assemble it yourself.

The Arduino board has its own processor and memory, is equipped with many inputs and outputs, to which various sensors can be connected, as well as actuators and mechanisms. At the moment, more than 20 major modifications of Arduino boards are available.

Why is the use of Arduino so popular?

The Arduino platform has been widely recognized by developers of new electronic devices, teachers, and students of engineering training areas, as well as schoolchildren in technical creativity circles.

Using Arduino simplifies the process of working with microcontrollers. In terms of technical equipment, it is ideally suited for the educational process of designing various mechatronic systems and robots, thanks to an understandable programming environment and the ability to observe physical processes in real-time, as well as an understandable programming environment and a number of other advantages.

It can be used as a means of training and research in digital signal processing, electronics, circuitry, robotics, automation, etc. More powerful Arduino boards are applicable for solving complex technical problems associated with the development of large projects and their complex automation.

Arduino is the most popular trend, making microcontrollers accessible to understanding and use by a large number of people, not even specialists in this industry. Using this popular platform, you can make a large number of interesting and useful projects.

We can say that Arduino is a universal extensible programmable controller-designer, which can become an indispensable assistant in solving any creative tasks related to random-use electronics, even an alarm clock, even a complex robot, even a stepper motor - all this, and not only, can control according to the desired algorithm using Arduino.

A huge number of all kinds of peripherals: buttons, sensors, LEDs, LCD indicators, and other organs of interaction with the outside world, are available for working with Arduino.

Hundreds of programs for Arduino are

already available on the Internet that can help both beginners and experienced users to implement their projects.

Chapter 1: Advantages and disadvantages of Arduino.

Advantages:

1. Arduino IDE is based on AVRGCC. Learning Arduino helps you learn C ++. If you don't like a specific high-

level command or library for Arduino, you can almost always replace it with a similar C ++.

2. You can power, program and exchange messages with Arduino using one USB cable (or FTDI cable for some clones).

3. You can make a simple project in a few minutes using standard libraries without delving into them. To read the signals of the buttons, display information on seven segments or LCD displays and control the engines for all this, there are standard libraries that do not require much programming experience.

4. Serial and SPI communication interfaces are made excellent.

Disadvantages:

1. Arduino IDE. The Arduino IDE is a cross-platform Java application that includes a code editor, compiler, and firmware transfer module to the board. This is the worst editor after notepad.exe. Someday you will switch to a more convenient third-party editor, but you still have to leave the IDE for the firmware.

2. Loader. To finish the project using Arduino, you will have to manually flash the boot loader in each new ATmega microcontroller. It takes 2Kb of memory.

3. A variety of options: in the official lineup there are options with a memory of 30 (32) KB and 254 (256) KB. What if your code takes, say, 42 KB? The only solution is to

use a semi-compatible clone of Sanguino et al.

4. Lack of a simple way to change the clock frequency. The 3.3V / 8MHz model can safely work at a frequency of 12MHz!

5. digitalWrite () uses 56 loops to execute. At least, you can easily find out the reason and switch to direct access to the port (the second thing that is replaced after the IDE). Arduino is not very convenient for time-dependent applications.

6. You cannot easily disable the standard library for serial hardware in order to take interrupts from TX and RX, regardless of whether it is running or not. A string is sent to the serial port using a state machine with many empty cycles for waiting for the buffer underrun flag in the

main body of the program - this is again a waste of resources - there are interruptions. Yes, you can enable interrupts in Arduino, but who does it?

7. Arduino libraries are easy to learn, but that is where their advantages end. For example, you can create delays all your life with the help of delay-functions and have no idea how the timer works on the microcontroller - all Arduino libraries consist of such minuses. After all, the timer and other peripherals in the microcontroller are implemented in such a way as to compensate for its single-threaded interruptions. And people spend CPU time decrementing an unused variable.

8. When the ISR timer overflows, an interruption occurs every 16K cycles in the background. This is done for the millis and micros functions, even when not in use.

9. An empty Arduino project takes 466 bytes on an Arduino UNO and 666 bytes on an Arduino Mega2560.

10. Also, Arduino "hides" such important aspects of the architecture of microcontrollers as registers, interrupts, and timers. Study them.

Chapter 2: Types of Arduino Boards

The Arduino team pleases us with new boards, periodically. Now there are a lot of them. Let us try to figure out what you need. As you know, Arduino was invented in Italy, they make original boards there.

The Italians themselves release the board in several basic form factors:

Ardino xxx - standard size, 20 I / O, full compatibility with all shields.

ArdinoMega xxx - oversized, 70inputs, not compatible with all shields.

ArdinoNano xxx - reduced size, 22 I / O, not compatible with shields.

ArdinoMini xxx - even smaller size, 20 input-output, not compatible with shields, does not have USB.

Arduino xxx Standard and most common size. When they say "Arduino" ("ordinary Arduino") - usually everyone immediately presents just such boards. The very first boards were in this form factor, so it was he who experienced the most reincarnations (USB versions in chronological order of exit):

Extreme, NG, Diecimila, Duemilanove, Uno, Leonardo.

You will not believe it, but a noticeable difference for the user is observed only in Leonardo. Now at the office. the site is offered for purchase only by Leonardo and Uno, however, the Internet is littered with the Duemilanove options (our CraftDuino is its kind, and for good reason - everything the average user needed was embodied in Arduino Extreme, since then very little has changed. All of these boards have the same number I / O, assembled on the same connectors (for connecting peripherals and shields), are programmed via USB, and have an ATMega microcontroller on board. In the early versions stood ATMega8, then they started to put ATMega168, then ATMega328. There are only 3 PWM outputs on the "eight", 8Kb per sketch 1Kb opera Attachment, but for many applications, ATMega168 already has 6 PWM channels and 16Kb for your needs, and the 328th 32Kb for programs and already 2KB of RAM. By the way, not all flash memory is available to the user, some of it takes up a bootloader. On all boards before UNO, there was a USB-UART FT232 converter chip, which allows you to plug the board directly into USB and program without a programmer. When you plug in the system, a virtual COM port appears, which is used by the Arduino development environment for programming.

1. Uno

At UNO, they decided to replace the USB-UART hard drive converter with an Atmega8U2 microcontroller (in later revisions 16U2) - a special firmware was uploaded to it, doing exactly the same thing as FT232.

What did it give?

The firmware speed has risen - now instead of 10 seconds you have to wait for 3c.

And most importantly, you can upload your firmware to this micro-converter and turn the Arduino into a mouse, keyboard or MIDI device, if you really need it.

Only this is being done, somehow not very Arduin-style, and there are still very few examples. This feature is not for beginners at all.

So, if your goal is to change the protocol for exchanging the board and computer, you want to make a keyboard-mouse-MIDI device (here, by the way, a MIDI console, on the most ordinary Arduino. Then, of course, you need UNO. And if you need you to have to write voluminous firmware for this (use large volume sources), then you need to look for the latest UNO revision - with Atmega16U2 (it has twice as much program memory)

Yes, it's worth mentioning here that this Atmega8U2 / 16U2 doesn't actually do exactly the same thing as FT232, it doesn't implement a very convenient feature - BitBang, so you won't be able to turn the board into a programmer in such a simple way.

Also, you should have noticed the

appearance of new pins on the UNO connectors. Yeah, they appeared - on the "upper left" connector - SDA and SCL - pins of the i2c interface, but they are duplicate (SDA and SCL and so are on 4 and 5 analog inputs) and this does not expand the functionality. Plus, the "lower left" connector has grown, the same 2 pins - standby and IOREF. The backup pin hangs in the air - it is not connected anywhere, and on the IOREF it is deafly planted at 5 volts (circuit). Someday this will probably come in handy ... but at the moment - old Shilds get into UNO, like native ones, new Shilds (of which there are still very few 1, 2 3 4), are fully compatible with old boards although they threaten to bury it with new pins - They may have to bend or bite.

Summing up my purely personal

opinion - there is no reason to chase just and only for UNO, except when you are going to rewrite the firmware of the USB-UART converter, and if you do not know what it is, then you definitely do not need any.

2. Leonardo

This is really a step forward - all on one chip, USB is independent of either UART or any kind of pin!

So, the board is built on the ATmega32u4 and has been pumped in comparison with previous models.

The RAM increased by 0.5 kB, there were 1 more PWM outputs, there were 12 analog inputs (6 are located where all Arduino boards are, the new +6 are scattered across digital pins) and, as already mentioned, USB and UART are separated.

It is also unpretentiously supported, not only the virtual com port but also the mouse and keyboard, which is much simpler than that implemented in UNO.

Well and, of course, a micro-USB connector.

True, "a step forward" came out with nuances - for a long time they struggled with various glitches and delayed the output, the pair still remained (tone and attachInterrupt functions), in addition, the bootloader now takes 4kb! And any USB sketch is shoved into any sketch for Leonardo - blink for Duemilanove / UNO will take 1084 bytes, and for Leonardo - 4858 bytes = \

Physically, Leonardo has the same wiring as UNO, so it is also compatible with old shields.

3. ArdinoMega xxx

A series of pumped boards (in size and characteristics) is represented by models (in chronological order): Mega, Mega2560 and Arduino ADK.

Almost all of the Shields are successfully plugged into the cards, but due to the different (with the "usual" Ardinos) pin layouts of the SPI interface, the Shields using it with digital pins 11,12,13 will not be compatible. An example is an old Ethernet shield. On the new SPI, it is taken from the standard ISP plug and everything works fine on both "mega" and "ordinary" Arduino.

There are a lot of conclusions on the boards:

54 digital

15 of them with PWM

16 - analog,

Memory pile:

128 / 256kb - flash,

8kb of RAM

4kb of its industry

and as many as 4 hardware UARTs!

The Mega is built on the ATmega1280, and the 2560 and ADK are on the ATmega2560, so motherboards with different memory sizes are different, moreover, on the fresh - 2560 and ADK - the USB part is made on ATmega8U2 (on later revisions 2560 - on ATmega16U2), here everything is like that of UNO.

And the ADK also has a USB-host, which

is expected to be a great friendship with Android phones.

4. Arduino nano

Small scarf with mini-USB. Shilds do not fit her, but she herself conveniently sticks into the breadboard.

Earlier versions used ATmega168, now they cost 328.

As a USB-UART bridge are FT232.

5. Arduino mini

Even less pay. (Yes, yes, exactly, there is some kind of historical blunder - an Arduino mini, for some reason it is much smaller than an Arduino nano.

I survived several versions - having insignificant differences in the purpose of certain conclusions.

It is not compatible with shields, but it is convenient for embedding in finished devices - nothing more.

There is no USB on the mini - it is programmed using the USB-Serial adapter (for example, based on the same FT232).

Also on the board is a very low-power stabilizer, and from the LEDs, there is only a power indicator and then on the latest versions.

There are board options that work at 3.3V and 8MHz, they used to set ATmega168, now they cost 328.

The Arduino project is completely open

(all the technical documentation necessary for production is available), and the boards safely copy and creatively process everything for everyone.

The restriction applies only to the name "Arduino" - it can not be used to call names of non-Italian boards (the Chinese, of course, spat, so more law-abiding manufacturers are scumbagging with derivatives, they have already come up with a lot, by the way.

Everything that non-Italians have bred can be divided into three groups: "clones", "compatible" and "Arduino-like".

Attention! It is important to remember that only original boards will open all the possibilities for you.

Since clones are fakes, we will not

mention them.

6. Compatible

These boards are very similar to and compatible with Arduino boards. This can be added to your project with Arduino.

For instance:

Freeduino

Freetronics Eleven

Seeeduino

Craftduino

Diavolino

Japanino

and many more.

As a rule, improvements and processing are quite aesthetic in nature (they do not carry fundamental changes in functionality or characteristics), otherwise the boards would lose compatibility. Typically, these are additional connectors, a different arrangement of LEDs and buttons, their own wiring, the use of other components (in other cases, other sizes), other power circuits, reset, USB parts.

I repeat, this class of boards is fully compatible with Arduino - and Shilds can be stuck and work with IDE as relatives. The most striking example - indicated at the office. the site of the Italians has the Arduino board (the power scheme is simplified and the USB port is removed) in fact they were invented and made by Sparkfun.

Naturally, they are not limited to the mainboard size - there are versions of mini- and nano- and mega-compatible processors, though in these cases compatibility is not such an important thing.

Here I am everything Taldych compatible incompatible; it's time to clarify what is meant.

Compatibility with Arduino consists of two things:

1.Compatibilities with boards with extensions - shields. To do this, the location and type of connectors should be like on the Italian Arduino Duemilanove / UNO. So, for example, the most Italian-original Nano is not compatible with shields.

Naturally, no one canceled the wires and tape - you can connect anything.

2. Software compatibility. (the program part of the Arduino project is a development environment (IDE), libraries and sketches)

Atmel motherboards are equipped with Atmel microcontrollers, ATMega families - ATMega8 / 168/328 - on all but Mega (ATMega1280 / 2560) and Leonardo (ATMega32U4).

Typically, these MKs are clocked with a 16MHz quartz resonator (Less commonly 8MHz)

MK feed on boards from 5V (less often 3.3V)

Sketches are downloaded through the bootloader (a special bootloader

ARDUINO

program previously flashed in MK), although in recent versions of the environment the option of flashing the sketch through the programmer has appeared, so this is probably not a criterion.

So, ANY board that satisfies these conditions (the type of controller, frequency, voltage, bootloader availability) will be able to use all the achievements of the Arduino community - both sketches and libraries, and you can write all this in the same Arduino environment, and load from there.

If you have straight arms, you can file libraries for use not in an Arduino environment or an environment for using boards with uncharacteristic Micro or frequencies of their work. But it seems like here beginners are being considered here - what are the edits of the environment and libraries ?!

So we will consider only those boards that work correctly without any additions as software compatible.

7. What kind of Arduino is necessary to have at home?

It all depends on the needs, I can give you only a couple of tips:

1. Be sure to purchase Arduino Uno, a convenient development board, great functionality, average price.

2. If you want to make a small device, for example, control of fluorescent lamps or a combination lock, then you will need to think about portable types of Arduino, Mini or Nano.

3. If you do not have enough resources

for your controller, then one option remains, this is Arduino Mega, it is also convenient for developing new projects, but in most cases, such computing power will not be needed for the first time.

All the "sizes" and types of Arduino boards are absolutely compatible with each other - if you are interested in a project on ArdinoNano - nothing will stop you from implementing it on a regular Ardino (Freeduino) or ArdinoMega (SeeduinoMega), and there's nothing to redo anything in the code in the circuit have to. It is possible and vice versa, for example, from "mega" to "mini" - if only there are enough conclusions/memory (often frankly redundant boards are used in projects), study the characteristics.

There is also no difference in choosing a specific board within the size range - we take a project for Arduino Diecimila (DFRduino) and calmly make it on UNO (CraftDuino) and vice versa!

Chapter 3: Arduino Mega Server

The secret is partly in supporting the Ethernet shield to connect an SD card up to 32GB. And partly in matching this monstrous volume for Arduino with software, which should allow the server to output data from an SD card at the request of the browser. It would also be nice to dynamically update files on the server so as not to shut down the server every time you want to change the background color of the start page from pale blue to turquoise.

This task (updating files, not changing colors) is assigned to the Arduino Serial Commander software, which pushes files into the server without stopping its operation.

Arduino Serial Commander

The task does not seem particularly difficult at first glance, then why was this done only now, at a time when the eight-bit MKs were almost extinct? Our version consists in one thing - in the stereotype of thinking. Ordinary programmers do not fit the concepts of "eight-bit MK" and "hosting", "HTML5", and other "goodies" of Arduino Mega Server'a.

This is not to say that there were no attempts, if you search, you can even find a server on the ATTiny2313 and ENC28J60, but all of them were timid and incomplete, and most importantly - scattered attempts. It is time to put it all together and get something on the edge of fantasy.

APPLICATION AREA

The technology, of course, is cool, but if it does not have a scope, then why should a primitive person have a computer? Fortunately, the Arduino Mega Server has an area for realizing itself and will become a good tool in good hands.

The word "Server" in the title does not necessarily mean a football-sized room, pushed by Arduino's, which runs on a dozen social networks from which you receive $ 10,000 per hour of work. I hasten to disappoint - the performance of the SD cards leaves much to be desired, so the Arduino is unlikely to surpass in this regard any, even the dead PC.

The main point of the system is different: with Arduino Mega Server (AMS) you can interactively control your microcontroller device, display beautiful control panels on the WEB, and the like. This approach, of course, will shock you first, and then the one to whom you are doing this project (or again you).

Also, in our opinion, self-documenting will be a worthy application of the system. For example, in your bunch of radio trash, you stumble upon an Arduino board half eaten by mice ... shake off a spider that settled there ... what does this Arduin'a do?

Of course, in antiquity you have lost all the manuals. With AMS, you simply connect the controller to the network, and he will tell you what, how and why he does it. Not only tell, but show!

One of the important functions of the project is also training, because the best training is work! Not just stupid and meaningless tasks like modifying Hello World'a, but doing real work! If you dig into the code, you will very quickly recognize the low-level part of the project, as well as the work of Arduino with the Internet itself, then high technologies such as JavaScript, CSS, HTML and many others are different!

Well, if you're not interested in the author's idea, you can simply copy and paste from the code the blanks you need to work with peripherals or something else.

1. Supported Web Technologies

Files without limits. There are no restrictions on the size and number of files. Content is limited only by the size of your memory card (up to 32 GB)

2. Dynamic interface

Instantly display the controller status on a web page and instantly respond to button clicks in the web interface.

3. Modern web technologies

All modern web technologies are supported: HTML, CSS, JavaScript, Ajax, etc.

4. Luxury conclusion

Data can be displayed using JavaScript libraries, including 3D: Processing, three.js and the like.

5. Change content on the fly

To update the content, you do not need to turn off the controller and remove the memory card

6.Adaptive design

Pages themselves adjust to the screen size of your device

The secret is partly in supporting the Ethernet shield to connect an SD card up to 32GB. And partly in matching this monstrous volume for Arduino with software, which should allow the server to output data from an SD card at the request of the browser. It would also be nice to dynamically update files on the server so as not to shut down the server every time you want to change the background color of the start page from pale blue to turquoise.

This task (updating files, not changing colors) is assigned to the Arduino Serial Commander software, which pushes files into the server without stopping its operation.

7. Basic set

All you need to start the Arduino Mega Server is an Arduino Mega controller, an Ethernet Shield network interface card and a microSD memory card

Arduino Mega Server currently runs on the following platforms: Arduino Mega (8-bit), Arduino Due (32-bit) and Genuino 101 (32-bit), Arduino M0 and esp8266 / esp32 (Wi-Fi)

8. Fields of application

- DIY platform

Arduino Mega Server is a great foundation for your DIY projects. It already contains a user-friendly interface and built-in support for many devices. You just have to connect the necessary equipment and slightly change the code for your tasks

- Standalone device

AMS can be the heart of a finished device, such as a weather station or security unit. The uniqueness of the technology lies in the fact that all the functionality is already contained inside the controller and such a controller can contain any number of devices. This is a clear embodiment of the 100 in 1 concept.

- Network station

AMS can act as a network device with virtually unlimited network capabilities. This is hosting a lot of sites, and interacting with their older and younger "brothers," and executing remote commands and issuing commands to other controllers on the network, and integrating with home automation systems and so on.

- Smart home controller

On the basis of AMS, a powerful smart home controller can be created with the broadest capabilities and unique consumer qualities.

- An educational and entertaining set

Arduino Mega Server is an excellent basis for a training or game kit for teaching programming, robotics, etc. for children and adults. The controller can contain extensive interactive documentation and ready-made examples of experiments, experiments, and finished devices, and to use this set you do not need in-depth knowledge of electronics and programming.

Chapter 4: Arduino IDE

The first, and often the only program for beginners to work with the Arduino controller is the Arduino IDE - an integrated development environment from the creators of the platform. You can download the main versions of this program on our website for free, just below are the download links. For your convenience, we have selected the most recent and popular versions of programs. In other materials on ArduinoMaster.ru, you can learn more about installing and configuring the Arduino IDE.

To get started, let's briefly find out what an IDE is and get answers to the most frequently asked questions. If you are an experienced developer, you can safely fly to the next section of the article with download links.

What is Arduino IDE?

The abbreviation IDE stands for Integrated Development Environment, in translation - an integrated development environment. Using this program, programmers write programs, and they do it much faster and more conveniently than using conventional text editors.

Within the Arduino platform, the Arduino IDE does the same — it helps programmers write programs. With its help, a sketch written in the Arduino language is checked, converted to C ++, compiled, loaded into Arduino. Theoretically, you can do without this program, but there are practically no other options for starting work with Arduino for a beginner. Therefore, the first thing you should do is find and install this programming environment for yourself. It is completely not difficult and absolutely free.

How to download and install Arduino IDE

The procedure for downloading and installing is absolutely traditional. You download the file, start the installation. On the official website, versions with the installer (exe) and regular zip archives are available. You can find versions of the Arduino IDE for all major operating systems.

The installation procedure is quite simple, you will need to answer a few questions. An important step in this process is to install the COM port driver. For most "Chinese" Arduino boards, you will need to install additional drivers.

After installation, you need a little setup of the environment - we'll talk about this in a separate article about installing and configuring the Arduino IDE.

Which version of the Arduino IDE to choose?

The first version of the Arduino development environment officially appeared in August 2005. Since then, a lot of water has flowed, the program has undergone revolutionary changes several times. Until 2011, version numbers consisted of one digit (the last was 0023 - version dated November 9, 2011). Then came the more familiar record with "minor" and "major" updates. So, Arduino 1.0.0 appeared on November 30, 2011, and version 1.0.1 - in May 2012.

Transitions from version 1.0.7 and 1.5 became the key ones in terms of the number of updates and related compatibility issues. Many libraries written under the "old versions" of the program could not be compiled into new ones due to changes in system libraries and other internal mechanisms for building the project. This was especially evident when switching to version 1.6. If your project has ancient libraries that do not work correctly with modern versions of the IDE, you will have to change them yourself, wait for the authors to do this or obey the circumstances, and install the version with which the library will work.

The latest stable version of the Arduino IDE at the time of writing is 1.8.7.

Download Arduino IDE from the official site

To download the program from the official Arduino.cc website, you need to find the Software - Downloads item in the site navigation. Find on the page links to the latest versions of the program (for Windows, Linux, Mac OS X). By clicking on the link you will be taken to the download page, where you can select the download option:

With project support (indicate how much you are willing to donate)

Without support. Just click on the "Download" button.

Regardless of the option selected, you still download the same version, there are no restrictions for the "free" version. But if you have the opportunity, then try to donate to the team that has done so much for the development of the project.

Arduino IDE Online

If for some reason you cannot or do not want to install Arduino on your computer, you have the option to create sketches in the online version. To do this, open the page of the online development environment on the official website of Arduino. Before you begin, you need to register, after which you can open the programming environment.

Chapter 5: Arduino projects that everyone must to try.

Arduino Microcontroller Process Automation Example

The simplest example of process automation can be the Arduino greenhouse. To create any system, it is necessary to clearly outline the tasks that it should perform. Using the example of a greenhouse, it will be:

1. Creating a special climate.

2. Timely on and off lighting.

3. Timely watering of plants and keeping air humidity at the same level.

One of the projects to create a greenhouse using Arduino

Based on these tasks, you can immediately notice what you need to buy to the mainboard:

1. The temperature sensor. He will make sure that the air does not heat up and cool down, being within the limits prescribed by the program. In case of temperature changes, the board will include air conditioning or electronic batteries.

2. Light sensor. Of course, you can limit yourself to a software solution and buy expensive lamps with imitation of daylight. But if you want to create a full-fledged greenhouse, then it will be much more convenient to install an automatic

ceiling, which will be controlled by Arduino.

3. Humidity sensor. Here everything is the same as with the temperature, according to the prescribed scenario, the board will include sprayers and humidifiers, if necessary.

When you purchase all the necessary modules, it remains only to program them. Indeed, without a code, these are just pieces of iron that are not capable of anything.

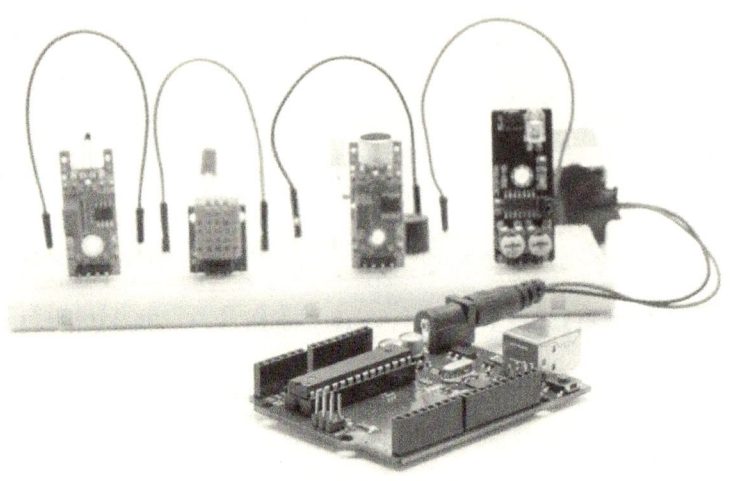

Arduino microcontroller programming for process automation. Example

As in the last paragraph, for programming, it is important to divide the task into separate sub-items and perform it sequentially. Arduino programming takes place thanks to the commands in the AT and AT + interface, using the prepared libraries. Accordingly, all scripts are written in a special environment in C ++ and, before doing anything, devote time to studying its semantics. In addition to performing simple functions, the system is also capable of storing scripts in flash memory, which is what we need in this example.

Do not forget that the information from each sensor comes in real-time and as variables, but you can limit the response time since there is no need to constantly spend resources and measure each parameter. Accordingly, set the time for each sensor to turn on and off, or set the response time for a certain period.

DIY thermal imager

A thermal imager is a device for measuring the distribution of surface temperature in a non-contact, visual way. As a rule, the temperature distribution map is displayed on the color display integrated into the thermal imager (or subsequent data transfer to a computer) as a color image, where red indicates the most high-temperature areas, and black or blue - low-temperature areas. Such devices are very expensive (several thousand dollars) and allow you to determine the temperature of dynamic (moving objects) in real time.

But, such functionality is not always needed. We describe the manufacturing process of a homemade scanning thermal imager, the cost of which does not exceed $ 200. The process of scanning an object takes about a minute. This thermal imager is suitable for shooting static objects.

The device uses two servos (for moving horizontally and vertically), an Arduino controller (for processing signals and transmitting data to a personal computer), a laser module or a laser pointer (so you can see the scanning area), the MLX90614ESF non-contact temperature sensor module, housing and rotary device.

List of used items:

MLX90614ESF-DCI or MLX90614ESF-BCI temperature sensor module:

Search MLX90614ESF on Aliexpress

futureelectronics.com ~ $ 47 (DCI version) or digikey.com ~ $ 37 (BCI version)

Arduino UNO (or equivalent) - $ 5

Housing with battery compartment for Arduino - $ 6.5

Servo motor (medium) - $ 11

Servo motor (large) - $ 13

Laser Card module - $ 8 (can be replaced with a laser pointer):

Search for a module on AliExpress, a module on Sparkfun

Webcam Microsoft LifeCam VX-700

Rotator (2 coordinates) Lynxmotion Pan and Tilt Kit:

Aliexpress 5-7 $, Robotshop.com 9.95 $, lynxmotion.com 9.95 $

MLX90614 Sensor

MLX90614 is an infrared thermometer in the TO-39 housing. Datasheet PDF.

Sensor data can be read using SMBus or PWM. In our case, a sensor with a DCI or BCI index is used. Power 3V. Index I denotes the type of form factor, I - with a nozzle to provide a narrow field of view of 5 °

Imager assembly

1. First you need to place the Arduino board in a case with a battery compartment

2. Using superglue or epoxy, fix the servomotor in the empty space in front of the Arduino.

3. Place the second servomotor in the rotary device and secure the entire structure to the servomotor.

4. Now, you need to connect the MLX90614 to the Arduino. To do this,

connect Ground to GND, Vin to 3.3V, SDA to pin 4 and SCL to pin 5. Also, install a 4.7 kΩ resistor from SDA to 3.3V, and the second from SCL to 3.3V.

5. Connect the Laser Card or laser pointer. A laser is needed so that you can see where the thermal imager is currently scanning.

6. After that, you must install the webcam and orient it precisely with the IR sensor and laser so that they are directed to the same point. This completes the assembly of the thermal imager.

Arduino Software

You need to download a sketch to configure the sensor. After uploading this sketch to Arduino, open Serial Monitor and press the key. The program will change the settings of the EEPROM sensor. This is required to be done only once. After you see "Finish", disconnect the Arduino from the PC and reconnect it.

And so you need:

Download the main working sketch of Arduino.

Additionally, I2CMaster library is required.

Computer software

The computer software is written in JAVA, so you will need the Java Runtime Environement. The software runs on Windows, Linux or Mac OSX in 32-bit & 64-bit. However, if it runs under Windows 64 bit, it is better to install a 32-bit version of JAVA.

List of Radio Elements

• Arduino Uno board 1 piece

• Temperature sensor MLX90614 1 piece (MLX90614ESF-DCI or MLX90614ESF-BCI)

- Resistor 4.7 kOhm 2 pieces

- Servo motor. It should be an average size of 1 piece.

- Servo motor. It must be a large size 1 piece

- Laser Card Module 1 piece

- Webcam 1 piece

RGB tape control from smartphone and Arduino

RGB tapes are capable of producing a luminous flux of any color, they usually use LEDs in the housing of which there are three crystals glowing in different colors. For their control, special RGB controllers are sold, their essence is to regulate the current supplied to each of the colors of the LED strip, therefore, the intensity of the glow of each of the three colors is regulated (separately).

You can do it yourself with an RGB controller on Arduino, even more so, this project implements control via Bluetooth. To control the tape, an additional 12V power supply is required, then the Arduino PWM outputs will control the gates of the field effect transistors included in the circuit. The gate charge current is limited by 10 kΩ resistors; they are installed between the Arduino pin and the gate, in series with it.

Remote control based on Arduino and smartphone

Using the microcontroller, you can make a universal remote control controlled from a mobile phone.

For this you need:

• Arduino of any model;

• IR receiver TSOP1138;

• IR LED;

• Bluetooth module HC-05 or HC-06.

A project can read codes from factory consoles and store their values. Then you can control this homemade product via Bluetooth.

Arduino face recognition and tracking system

In this project, we combined a face detection detector and a tracking system.

Briefly, the essence of the project: a webcam mounted on a swivel mechanism is connected to a computer running the Windows operating system and with OpenCV software installed. If the program detects a face in the field of view of the webcam, then the center of the face is calculated. X and Y coordinates are transferred to the Arduino controller, which is connected to the computer via USB. In turn, the Arduino controller controls two servo motors according to the received commands: in the X coordinate and in the Y coordinate, that is. A tracking system is provided.

Open Source Computer Vision Library is multi-platform, currently exists under the following OSs: Windows, Linux, Android, Mac OS, and even iOS. The library provides real-time image processing. It is written in C / C ++.

Thus, this project is a mixture of soft and hard solutions. Image processing is carried out on a computer, and the servo is controlled by a controller.

Software:

Arduino IDE 1.0 for Windows

OpenCV 2.3.1 SuperPack For Windows

Microsoft Visual C ++ 2010 Express SP1

Serial C ++ Library for Win32 (by Thierry Schneider)

Equipment:

Windows 7 SP1 computer

Arduino Uno or compatible + PSU

2 servos

USB webcam

Now step by step:

Step 1. Software Installation

1) If you have Windows, then download the OpenCV-2.3.1-win-superpack.exe file (or a later version) and install the library.

2) Download and install Microsoft Visual C ++ 2010 Express. If you have a 64-bit version of Windows, you will also need to download the Windows SDK (but for version 64 there may be problems).

Read the process of setting up OpenCV for Visual C ++ on the official website.

Step 2. Mounting the camera and servomotors

We attached the webcam to the X-axis servomotor, and it, in turn, fixed it to the Y-axis servomotor. And secured this entire structure to the "third-hand" clamp.

Step 3. Connection

Servo connection:

The yellow pin from the X-axis servo is connected to pin 9 of the Arduino controller

The yellow pin from the Y-axis servo connects to pin 10 of the Arduino

Red Vcc pin from servo connects to 5V pin

The black GND pin from the servo is connected to the GND pin of the Arduino controller.

Webcam connection:

The webcam is connected to the computer via a USB interface. The C ++ program identifies the webcam by its USB port number. You may need to specify the port in the program.Connect Arduino UNO controller:

The controller also connects to the computer via the USB interface. A virtual COM port appears in the system, which must be added to the C ++ program code.

Dynamic (swivel) webcam on Arduino

Let's try to install a webcam on a servo installed in the frame from the designer and control it using Arduino.

Recently, we were puzzled by the question of how else can I use the Arduino besides flashing LEDs.

Constructor frame

The first thing you need to do is the wireframe. For this, you can use parts from a metal designer and the like. In general, use your imagination.

Servo shaft connection

To connect the servo shaft with the gear, we used cold welding. we chose a cruciform gear on the shaft, because I practically do not need it for future projects, unlike other parts received with the servo drive.

You need to install it exactly right. we did it with a level. We were lucky that the distance between the sides of the frame was almost the same width as our servo. You can attach the servo to the base with double-sided tape.

I used a Logitech webcam. It would probably be useful to remove the counterweight from it to make it easier. This will facilitate the rotation of the camera.

Weight distribution

We added 2 thick gaskets to avoid shaft pressure on the chamber. They shift the weight of the camera to the entire frame from the servo shaft.

The webcam mounting element consists of a circle with a hole aligned with the shaft in the center. This allows traction between the shaft and the circle.

Some space is created by a gasket that prevents pressing on the shaft.

Problems:

- The camera is not fixed in the frame, and it will fall if it is tilted as much as possible.

- The holes in the designer above the servo drive are large, and allow the servo drive to make significant horizontal movements due to the load.

- The torque of the camera causes excessive rotation, which in turn deforms the servo drive. we want to try to fix it by rotating the camera 1 degree back after a period of continuous movement, but we prefer mechanical solutions. Perhaps this can be corrected by adding the transmission and installing the webcam on a separate belt-driven shaft?

- ... Or use a more powerful servo.

Electronics

Servo and LED connection

The servo drive has 3 wires:

- GND

- + 5V

- signal

I used 9 pins to control the servo.

The LED is connected to + 5V and GND with a resistor on the + 5V line and will glow when power is applied.

The program for Arduino, like all project files, can be downloaded below or taken on github.

The program allows you to control the web camera using USB and a joystick.

You can use modem control / terminal emulator applications such as Minicom or Putty to communicate with the USB port.

Center Installation:

- The program will set the servo at 90 degrees at startup.

- And when you press "m"

Left and right

- When the joystick moves horizontally.

- Left when pressing 'F'

- Right when you press "J"

Node.js

In addition, we implemented a web server in node.js to facilitate control over arducam.

The instructions can be found on the gihub project website.

Possible improvements:

- Ensure that the camera is rotated with the arrow buttons.

- Make a turn 1 degree back to ease the load on the servo that occurs when the torque of heavy web cameras.

Smart socket on the example of a teapot

When once again I had to get out of the chair and go to turn on the kettle, my friend jokingly said that you need to make a smart kettle that will turn on in voice. It will work like this: A person who wants to heat the kettle opens the application on the phone, pronounces a voice command, after the phone sends the command to the circuit board, which in turn turns on the relay and the kettle heats up, because we didn't want to open the kettle and build a relay in it, we made a socket with a relay module, which is controlled by the Arduino uno microcontroller.

To create such a system you will need:

• Arduino UNO

- Relay module

- Bluetooth module HC 06

- Bread board

- Wires for connection

- Extension cord, in which we will introduce relays with a plug and socket

About Bluetooth: The default PIN code 1234 is used to connect to it; AT commands are used to change it. Note: when connecting to the board, it is important to remember that TX on the module is connected to RX on the board, RX on the module is connected to TX on the board.

To control using a smartphone, you need a program that will send text via bluetooth to our microcontroller, to create such a program we used the MIT app inventor, here is the finished installation apk file for android: Teapot beta.apk, this program works like this: At the click of a button, it is read voice, the program compares the received text, if it matches the established commands, the smartphone sends a digit to the connected bluetooth.

The program on the microcontroller works like this: It constantly reads messages on the port and if the message matches the key, the board closes the relay.

For those who assembled such a device, I explain the commands:

• Heat the kettle - closes the relay, respectively, the kettle begins to heat up

• Turn off the kettle - the relay opens, as you understand the kettle stops heating

If you forget these commands, the program has a Help button, where all these commands are described.

Radio on Arduino

We will need:

Arduino Nano, namely version 3.0 (based on the Atmega328p microcontroller) -

 USB to UART converter on the CH340 chip. This option is cheaper than in comparison with FT232, but we don't see any problems, only other drivers need to be installed - special for CH340 / 341

So, to work with Arduino, we need to install Arduino software, through which we can write the firmware code (firmware for Arduino is called a sketch) and load it into the microcontroller in the same click. The firmware occurs through UART (for which a USB - UART converter is needed), this is a feature of the Arduino platform, which allows you to record sketches without a programmer. It is actually convenient, but also fast enough. On the whole, Arduino gave me the impression that it's all exactly the same as just AVR microcontrollers, only everything is renamed and presented in a different form. By the way, sketches are compiled with the help of the same sacred GCC, although the language for writing programs is slightly modified, it is already not C, but everything obeys the laws of the programming language C, C ++. The software interface is extremely minimalistic, it works smartly, performs its functions well, but no longer needs to.

Thus, in order to test the Arduino platform, it was decided to create a small project, namely a radio controlled via a personal computer. As a result, a circuit was born, according to which we assemble the device:

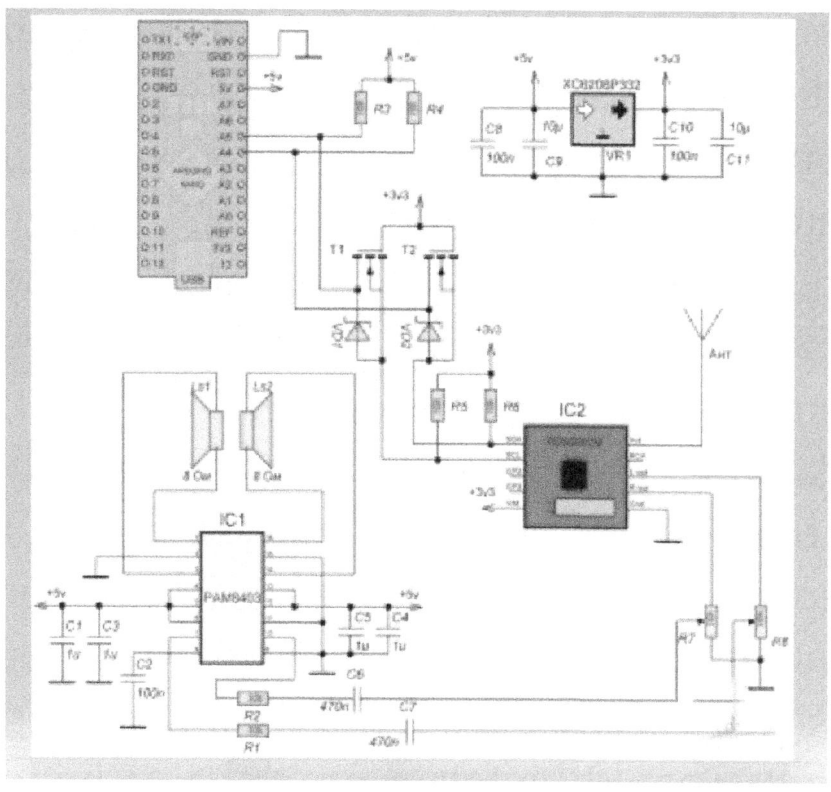

It is immediately worth noting that, if desired, the scheme can be minimized. The circuit is based on the Arduino Nano 3.0 board. It also has a microcontroller itself and a USB interface for connecting to a computer based on the CH340 chip. This will allow us to exchange information with a computer. Next, we used the I2C level matching module for safe operation with the RDA5807M radio module, which operates on a voltage of 3 (3.3) volts. In addition to transistors, a voltage regulator of 3.3 volts is located on the I2C level matching module, so this stabilizer is also present on the circuit. Another option may be to use simply transistors to match the levels, or use a specialized chip, such as PCA9517 or similar. Then the VR1 voltage regulator can be excluded from the circuit, and 3.3 volts should be taken from the Arduino board. Resistors R3, R4 and R5, R6 are necessary for the correct operation of the I2C interface, forming a high level on the data lines. Denomination can be varied within reasonable limits. As you can clearly see, the module based on the RDA5807M is used as an FM tuner. Here, at least in my case, in urban conditions (a lot of noise from household appliances, concrete walls, and so on), an antenna is needed long enough to receive the signal more confidently, in addition, it is advisable to place such an antenna closer to the window, for example, so that the signal is caught least drowned. The audio output of the radio module is connected to the audio amplifier on the PAM8403 chip. This is a D-class amplifier, power up to 3 watts. The sound quality is pretty good. The audio amplifier circuit is built in accordance with the datasheet. In addition, a ready-made module can be purchased (as in the photo) and used in the construction of such schemes. The module is assembled in the same way.

Variable resistors R7 and R8 control the volume level, it is desirable to use generally one dual resistor. Speakers are best used with a resistance of at least 8 ohms so as not to overload the USB port of a computer or laptop. With a load of 8 ohms, according to the datasheet, the output power will be 1.4 - 1.8 W, which fits into the standard power of the USB port. Although, on this account, one can object to the fact that modern computers have long come out of the 500 mA framework per port and can actually produce more. When you connect speakers with a resistance of 4 ohms, the output power will be 2.5 - 3.2 W, which, taking into account the consumption of the entire circuit, will not fit into 500 mA.

When assembling the layout due to the lack of a second speaker, only one right channel of the audio and, accordingly, one variable resistor was used to adjust the sound.

Since the circuit is configured using software on a computer, then the amplifier with speakers can be thrown out of the circuit and connected either directly to the speakers, or through the audio jack connect to the input of the computer's audio card (usually an input for a microphone) and allow the sound to be output to the speakers in the settings . You can choose any convenient way for you to receive sound from the radio. If you connect to the speakers, the resistors that control the volume of R7 and R8 can also be excluded, since the volume is controlled either on the speakers themselves or through Windows. The third option is to adjust the volume level through the settings of the radio module, but so far this function is not in the software.

Software needed to search for radio stations

The Arduino board is connected via a USB - UART converter (it is already part of the Arduino board).

In the program, accordingly, there are settings for selecting a COM port. Search for stations is carried out by the slider. UART data is transmitted as a channel number for the radio module. Having received this data, Arduino saves the last received radio channel to the EEPROM memory and the next time it is turned on, the parameters stored in the non-volatile memory of the microcontroller are used. That is, you can set up your favorite station once through a computer (if you are suddenly a fan of listening to the radio) and turn it on without it - the last station will always be saved. The program is written in C # in Visual Studio using Windows Forms.

In this development, the goal was not to make something super functional, but rather some experience working on the basis of Arduino with all the ensuing consequences.

The article is accompanied by a sketch for Arduino, an FM program for tuning stations, video of the device.

DIY crafts garland on address LEDs with your own hands

How about recharging the New Year's mood and making a garland with your own hands that can surprise not only you, but also your guests?

Let's not waste time, right to the point. The task of the project is to work independently and switch effects and create a New Year mood, so to speak against the background. we will make a garland, which in its essence will be similar to the well-known Twinkly Strings Smart-garland, similar to the fact that each bulb lives its own life, which allows you to display effects that are not available to ordinary Chinese garlands with a fixed set of colors.

May need

Altimeter GY-BME280.

High voltage module for electronic lighters.

Voltage stabilizer AMS1117.

DIY kit for the manufacture of electronic watches.

Mini circular saw, suitable for wood, metal, tile.

The New Year's model is based on address LEDs in the form of such modules on wires:

The control of such a tape is carried out using a microcontroller, you can use, for example, the Arduino Nano platform.

You can also use just such a tape, with round modules.

You can also buy a fresher version, it is made of transparent modules and the light from such LEDs will look more "cool".

Total for the repetition of this project will need:

- Arduino Nano;

- a small button;

- a 220 Ohm resistor, optionally, but still desirable with it;

- plug from the kit with a garland;

- power supply 5V, 2A;

- actually the garland itself.

The connection of all components will occur according to the following scheme:

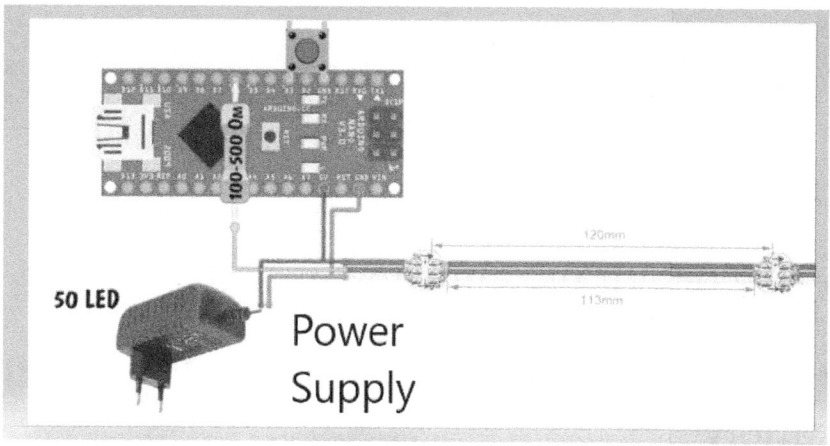

We start with the button. It can be soldered directly to the Arduino board. Next, we solder the plus (+) and the power supply ground of the tape, and the signal wire with a resistor. You can put this whole thing into heat shrink or wrap with electrical tape. Then we connect the controller to the computer, download the archive with the firmware. Install the necessary programs and libraries, and open the firmware file.

.You can customize:

• change the number of LEDs in the tape.

• Use or not use button controls.

• Current limitation from the power supply.

• Effect settings.

By default, sequential switching of effects is used, but you can make your own list of effects and switch them by it. Press the "Download" button and the firmware is loaded into the board. To power one segment of the garland, which is 50 LEDs, a power supply unit with a current of 2A will be quite enough, that is, even a charger from a smartphone is quite suitable. We solder it to power and pull everything into heat shrink or electrical tape. Everything, the garland is ready.

A single click on the button turns the garland on or off. By holding the button, the brightness level is adjusted, hold - increases, hold again - decreases, and so on.

Double click to turn on the next mode, triple-click to turn on the previous mode. This firmware version has about 40 modes. A fourth click turns the flash effect on and off.

That's all, actually - the main source of the New Year mood is ready. The garland looks very cool, the effects are mostly pretty interesting, but some honestly do not look very good, and it's not entirely clear what they really are.

In any case, this creation looks much more elegant than a usual garland.

LED mood cube

May need

5630/5730 LED chip for electronic home-made products.

Screwdriver, 25V.

JET JWDP-12 boring machine (All tools)

TM1637 7-segment LED display module.

Board Adjustable Power Supply DIY Kit.

Tools and materials:

- WS2812 LEDs - 96 pcs.;

- Printed circuit boards - 6 pcs.;

-Arduino Nano;

- Power supply 5V 1A;

-Soldering supplies;

-Computer with software;

-Iron;

-3D printer;

Step One: Plan

In our project, we use WS2812 addressable LEDs. The LEDs are connected in cascade, which means that you can control as many LEDs as you need with just one signal line / wire from the microcontroller. This makes wiring much easier.

ARDUINO

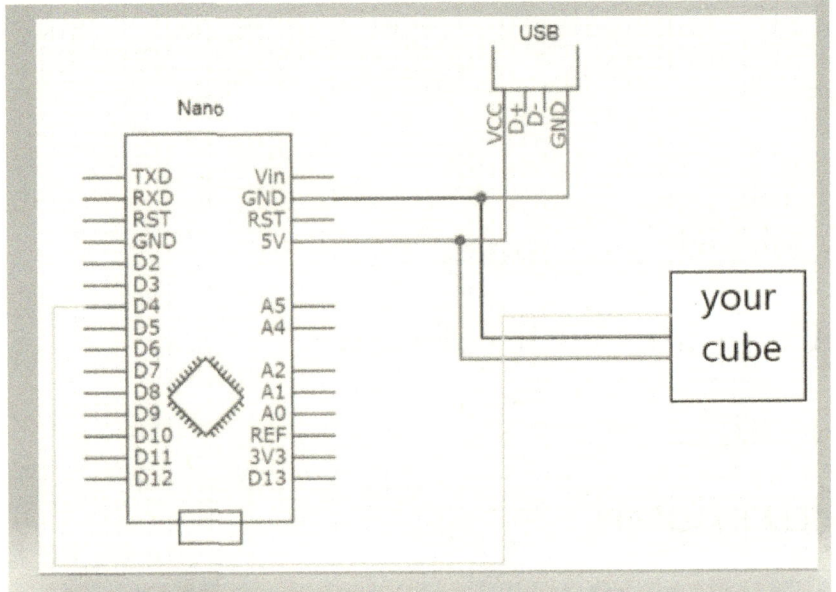

LEDs will be controlled by Arduino Nano.

Step Two: PCB

For the design of the circuit board, we used the EasyEDA program, as it is suitable for beginners.

The LED has 4 contacts:

VDD - 5 V

DOUT - output signal

VSS - Earth

DIN - input signal

As mentioned earlier, the LEDs are cascaded, which means that the signal comes from the microcontroller to the first LED on the DIN pin. From the DOUT pin, the signal goes to the DIN pin of the second LED.

When designing printed circuit boards, we planned to solder them manually, so between the LEDs, he left enough space for a soldering iron.

We didn't make the board ourselves but ordered.

Step Three: Board Mounting

First, we started manually soldering the LEDs one by one with a soldering iron. The result was not very good, not only was soldering the installation of 96

LEDs a laborious process, but they also overheated when soldering. Then we decided to go the other way.

The most widely used method for soldering SMD components is called Reflow Soldering. In this method, solder paste (a mixture of solder and flux) is applied to the pads on a printed circuit board and the components are placed on it. The solder paste is then melted or "melted" by heating it in a reflow oven. This is a quick and accurate method, if everything is done correctly. But using this method means that you need a reflow oven

Step Four: 3D - Print and Build a Cube

To assemble the cube, we first printed the parts on a 3D printer. You need to print the frame and six panels and the base details.

Now you need to glue the boards to the panels, and install the panels in the openings of the frame. To make installation.

Step Five: Arduino

Next, we connect the cube to the Arduino and the power supply.

Step Six: Code

Next, you need to install FastLED using the dispatcher. Open DemoReel100 from sample sketches. File> Examples> FastLED> DemoReel100.

Before downloading the code, make the following changes:

Define DATA_PIN (the pin on the Arduino to which the DIN cube is connected) to the one you selected. In this case, digital contact 4.

Define LED_TYPE as WS2812.

Set NUM_LEDS to 96.

And, click Upload.

Now you can enable the cube.

Conclusion

Arduino is constantly releasing new products. in our book, only a small drop of everything that you can do on this popular platform is considered. In fact, it all depends on your imagination and the task that you set for yourself. Arduino is an excellent solution for use in robotic systems. This allows you to perform the simplest tasks of managing a simple robot. In complex robots, it can be used to control individual parts by commands from the host computer.

I hope, that you really enjoyed reading my book.

Thanks for buying the book anyway!

Made in the USA
Monee, IL
02 December 2021